I0446974

THIS BOOK BELONGS TO:

....

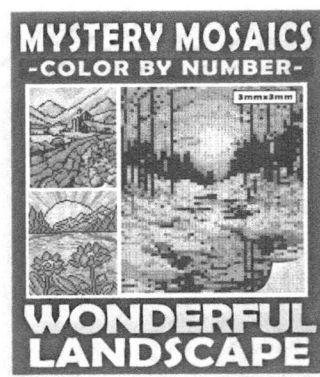
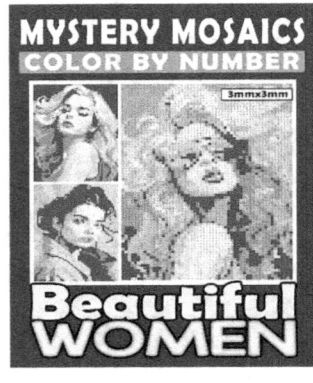
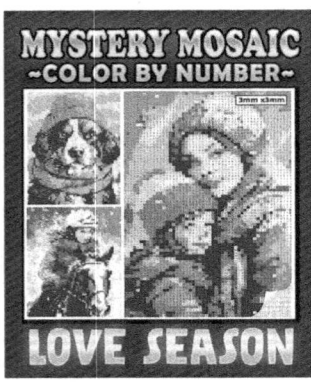
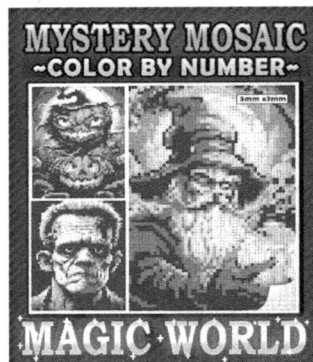
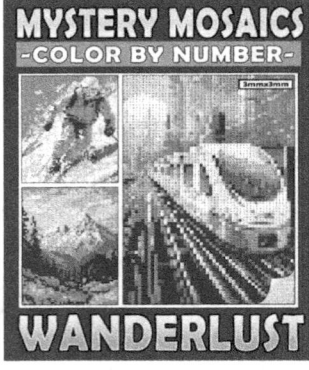
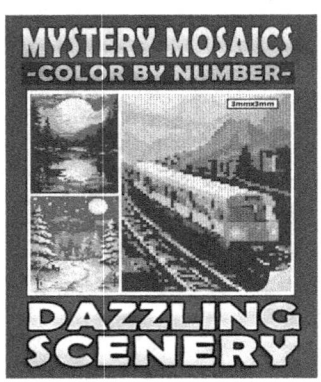
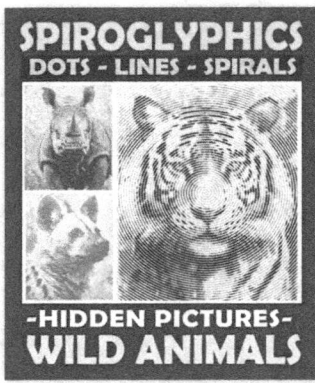
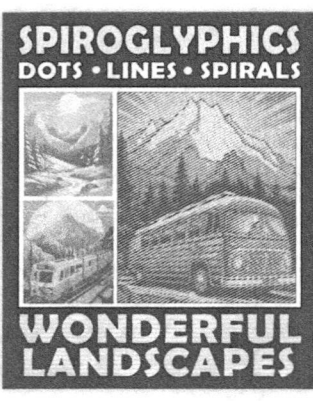
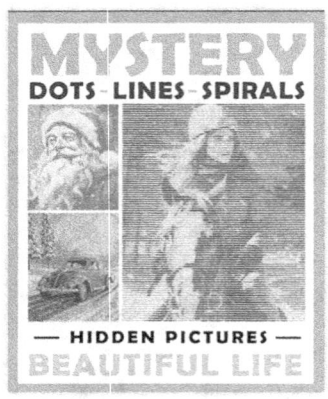
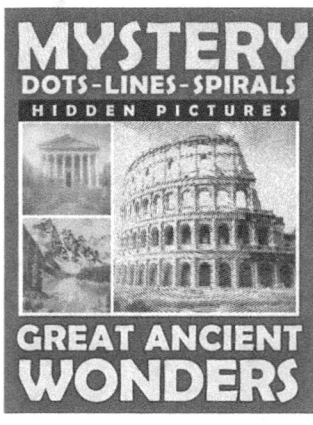
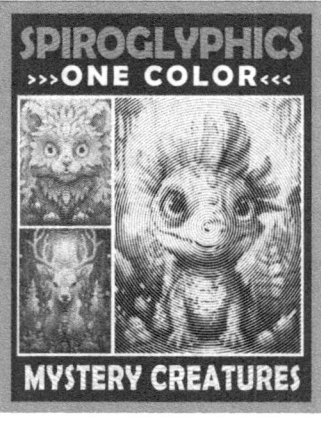
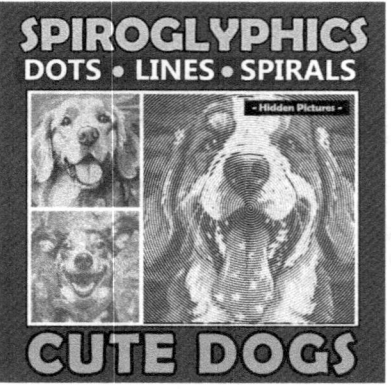

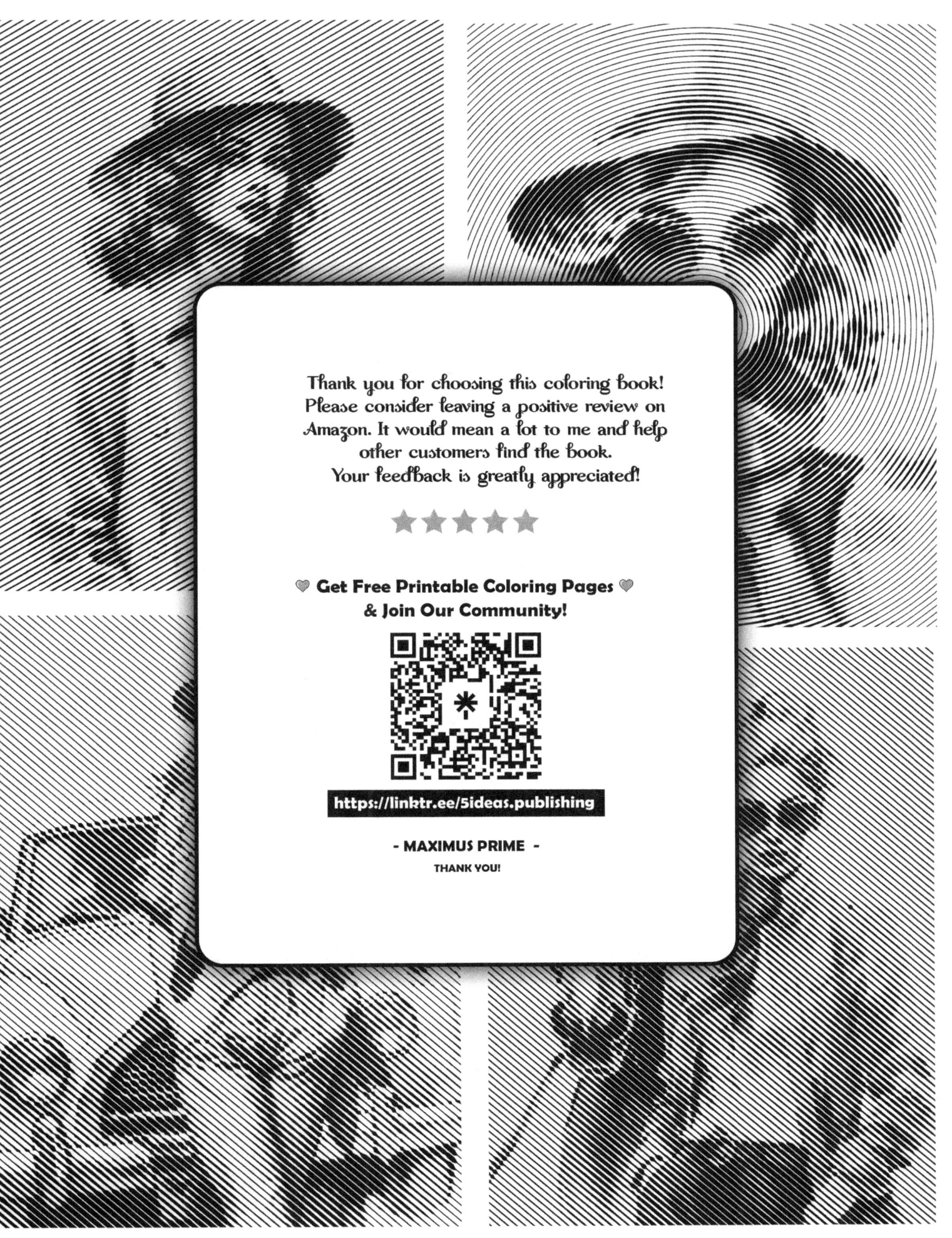

Thank you for choosing this coloring book!
Please consider leaving a positive review on
Amazon. It would mean a lot to me and help
other customers find the book.
Your feedback is greatly appreciated!

★★★★★

♡ **Get Free Printable Coloring Pages** ♡
& Join Our Community!

https://linktr.ee/5ideas.publishing

- MAXIMUS PRIME -

THANK YOU!

Where to start coloring?

For the spiral coloring pages
Start coloring by filling the lines from inside as shown here

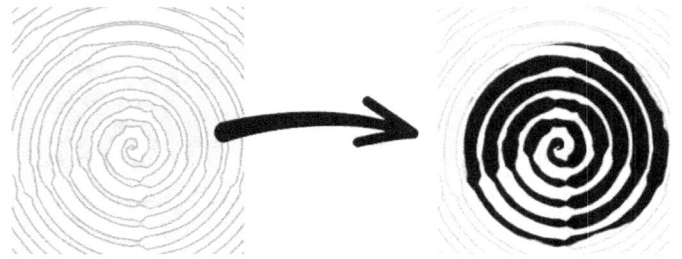

For the lines coloring pages:
Start coloring by filling the lines from upper lines
or the lower lines as shown here.

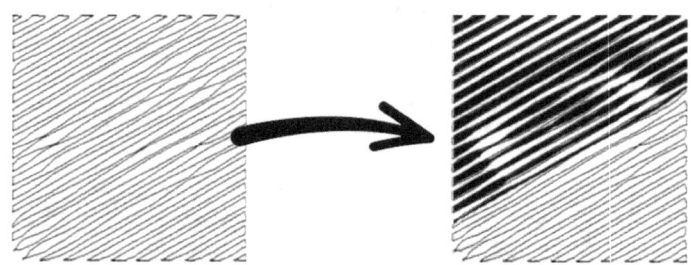

For the dots coloring pages:
Start coloring by filling inside the dots.

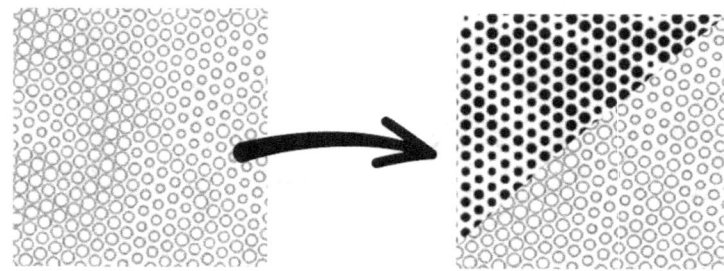

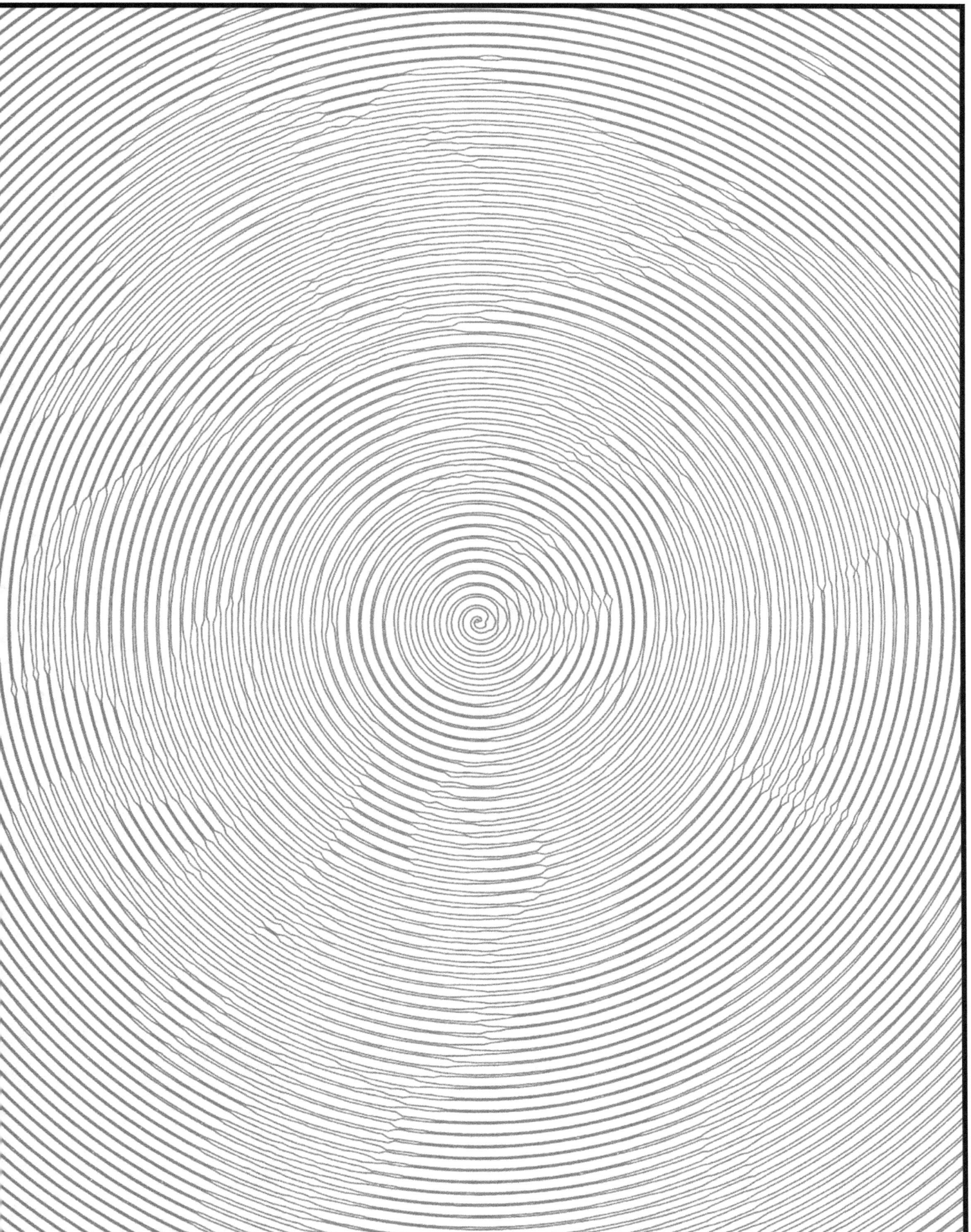

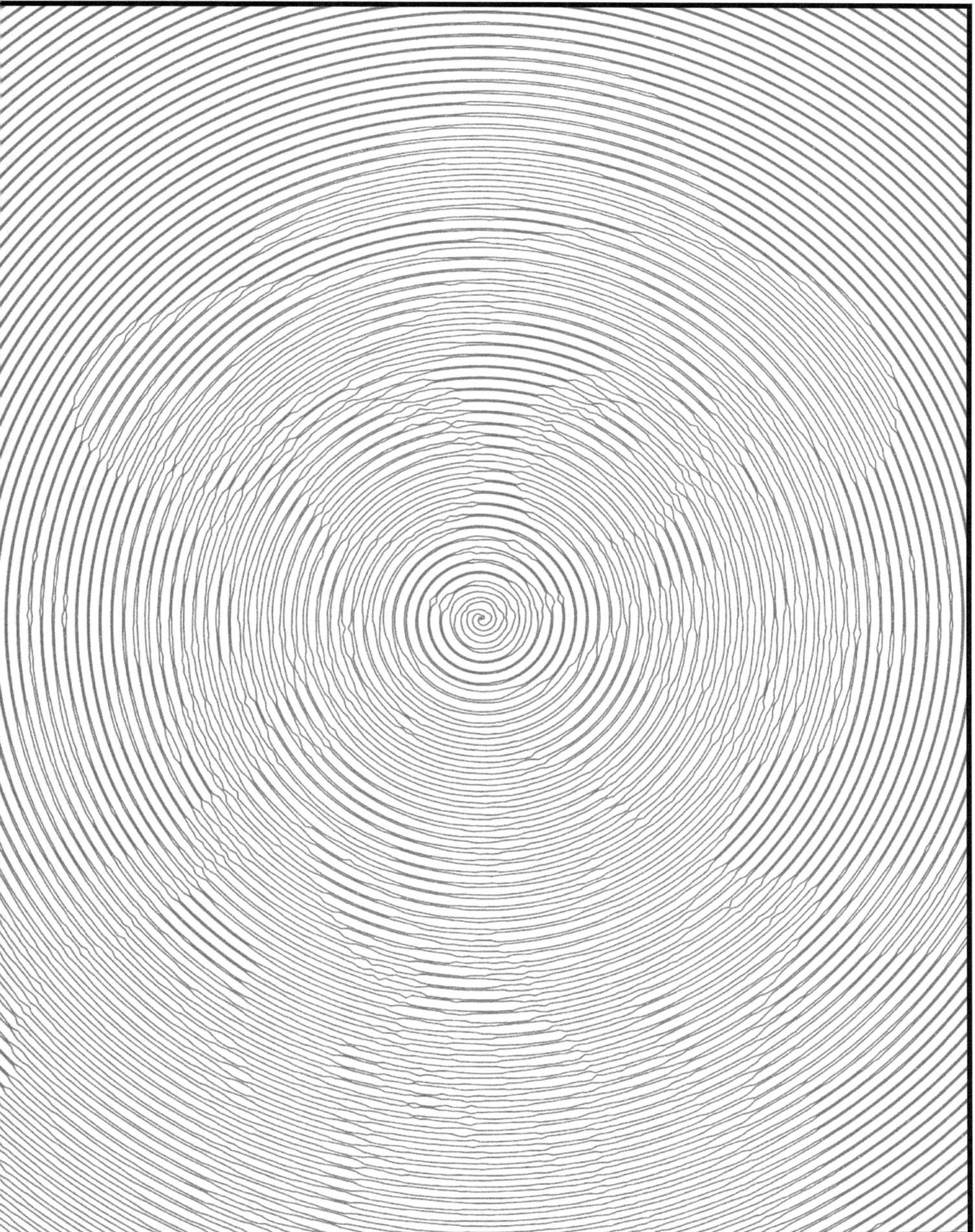

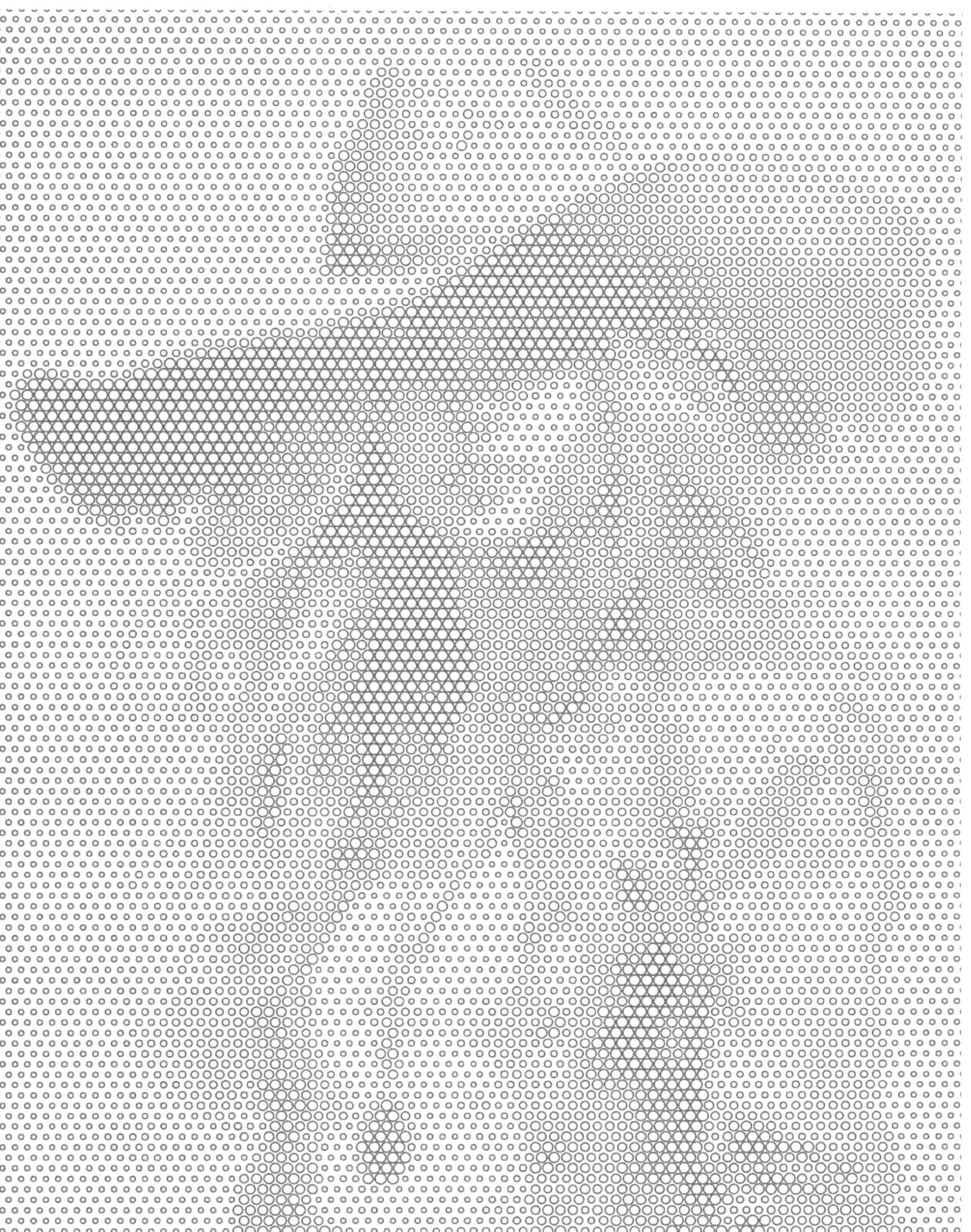

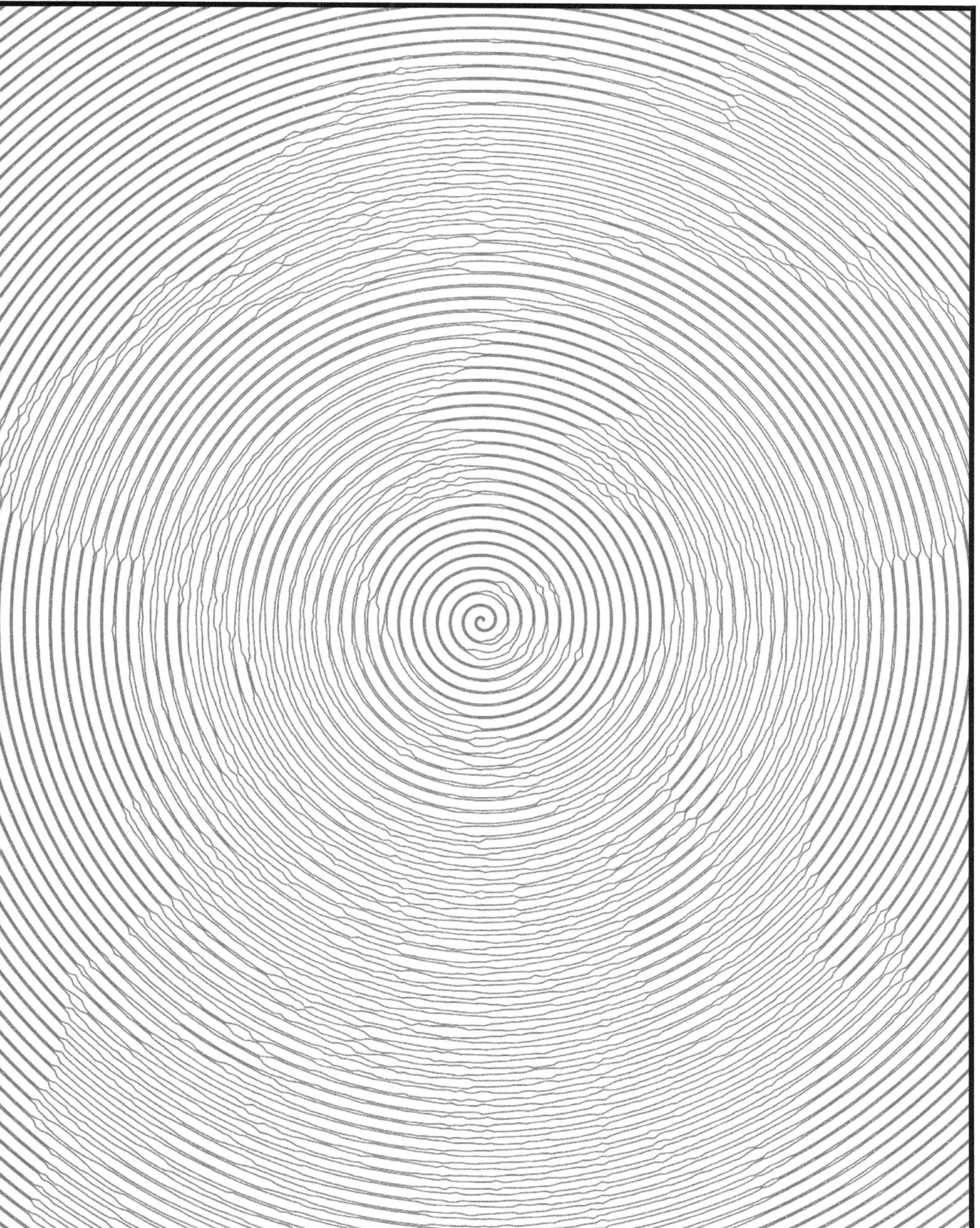

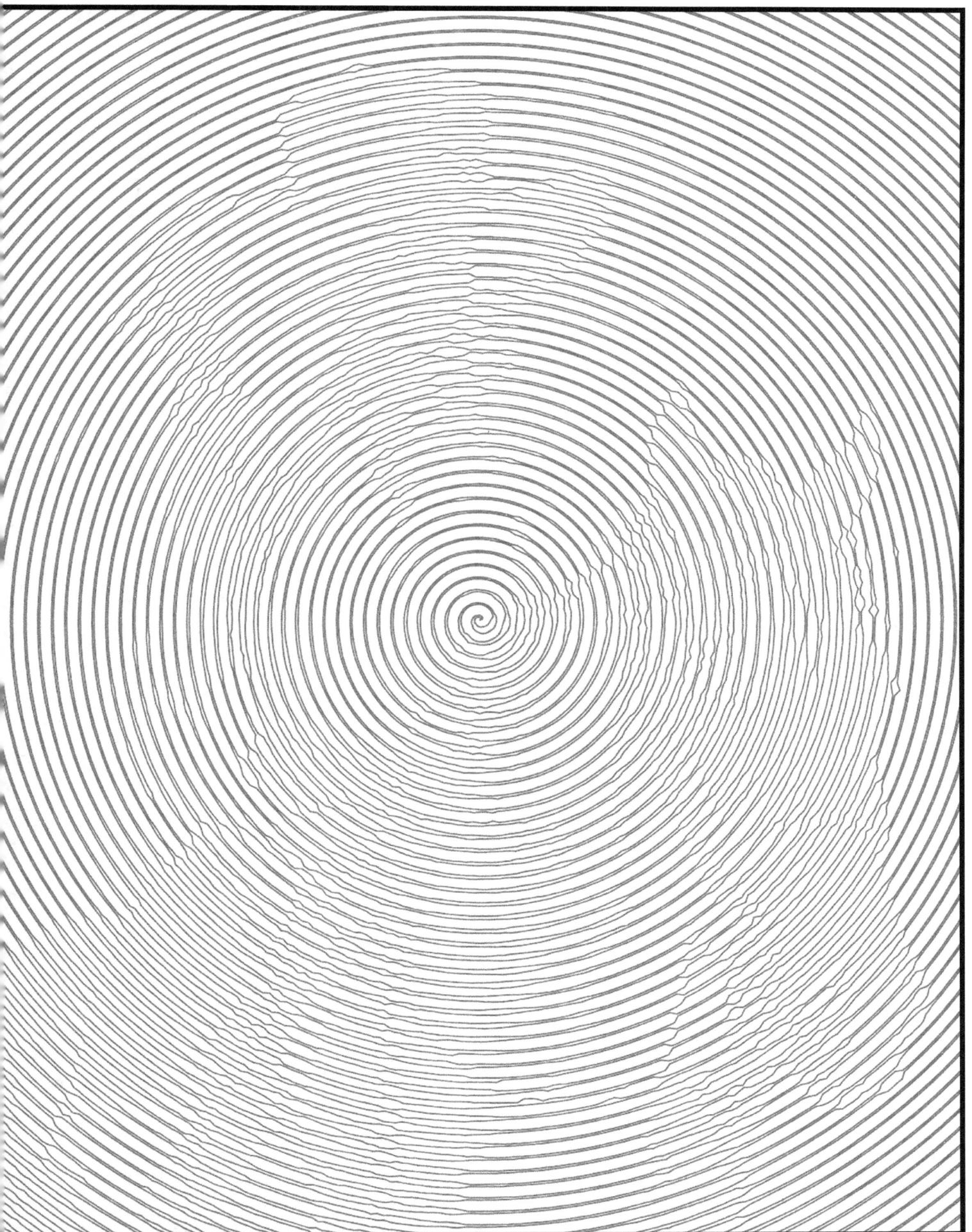

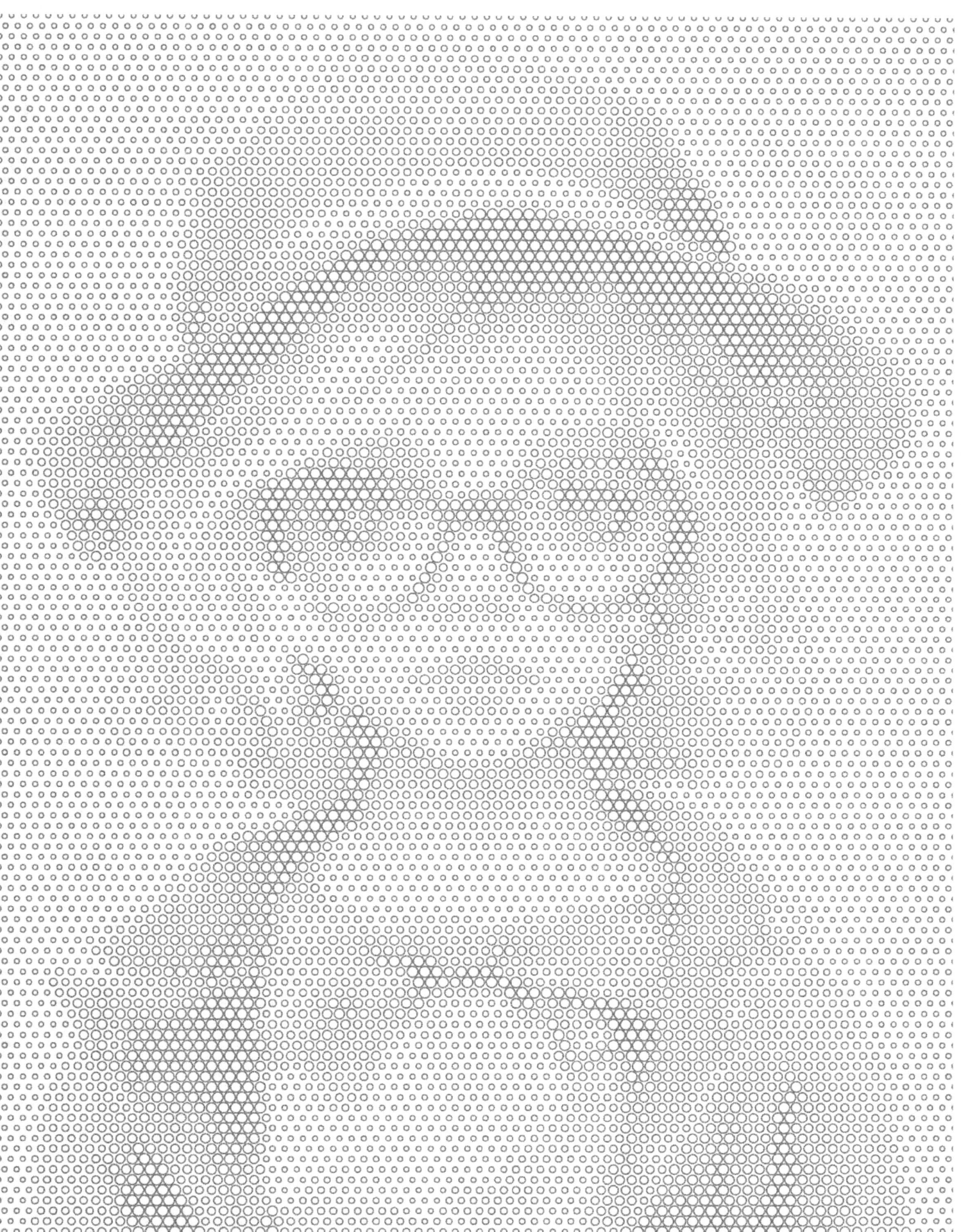

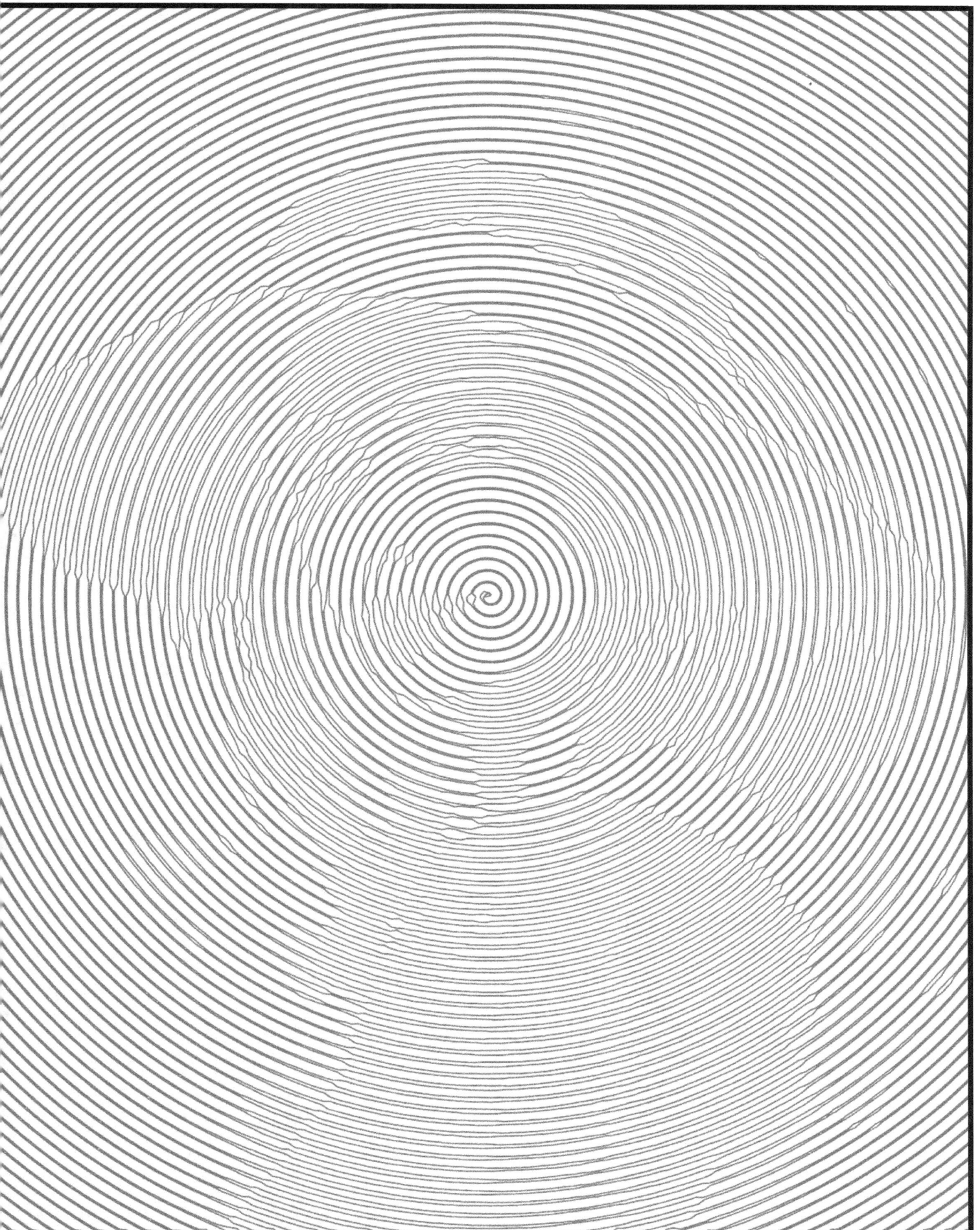

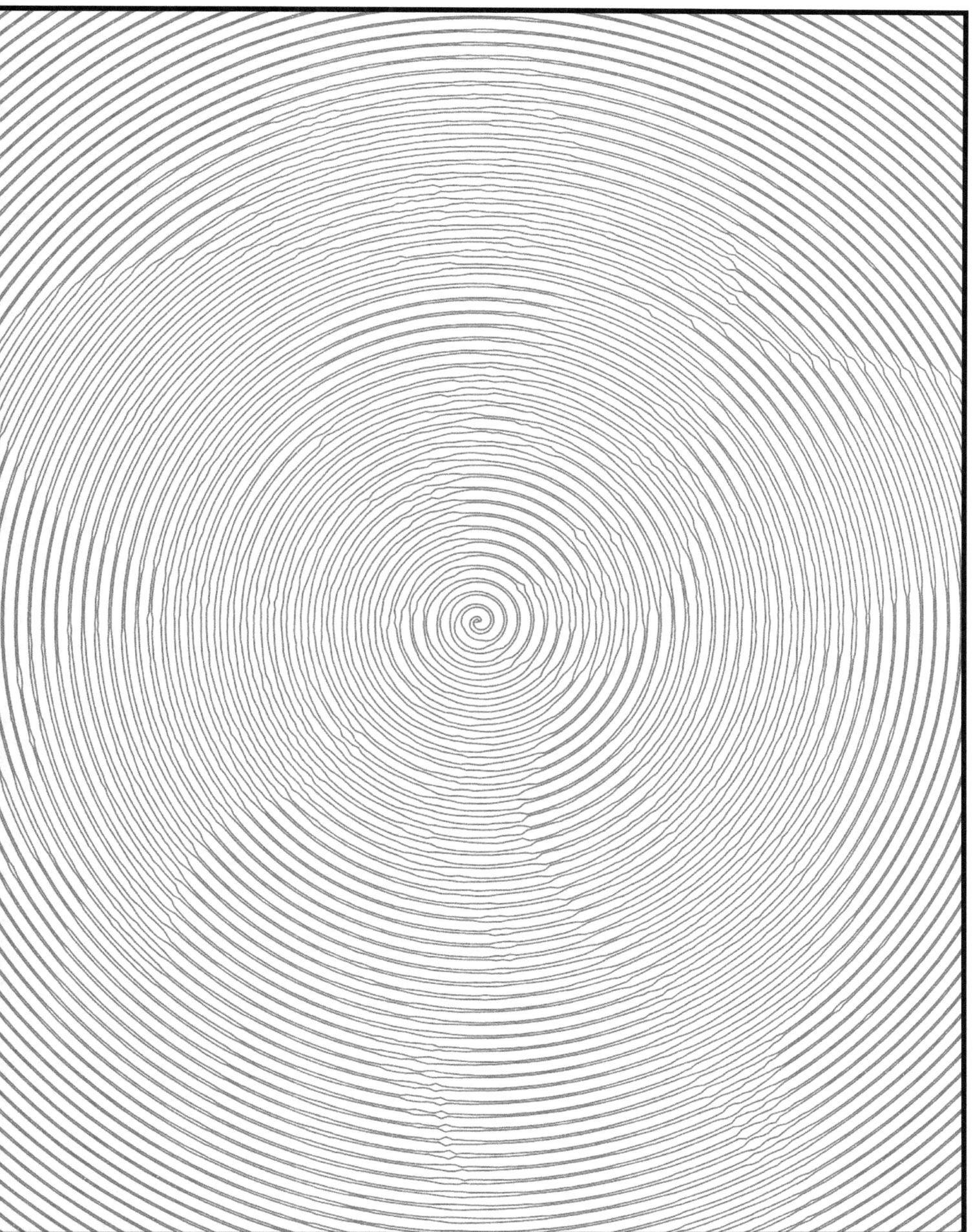

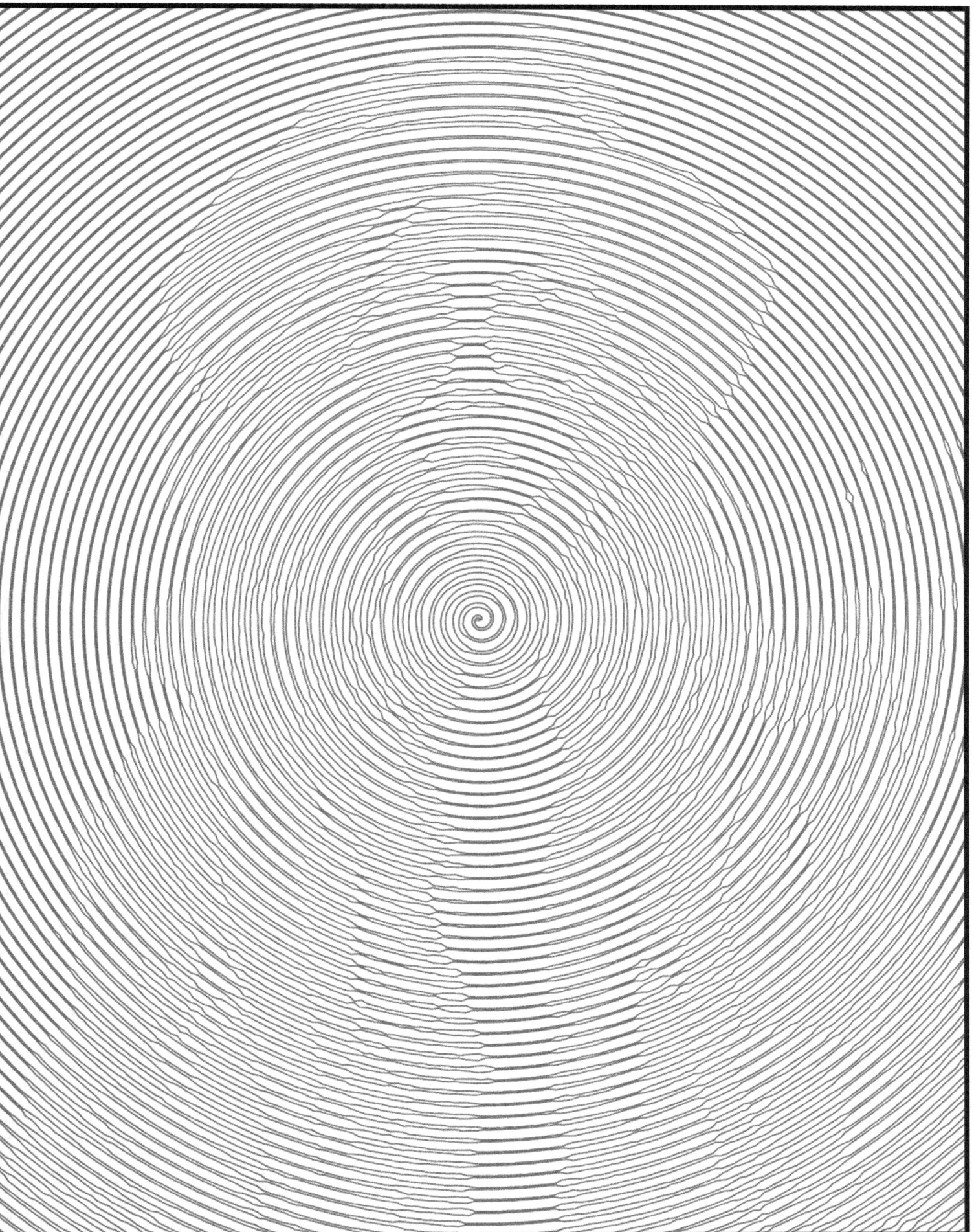

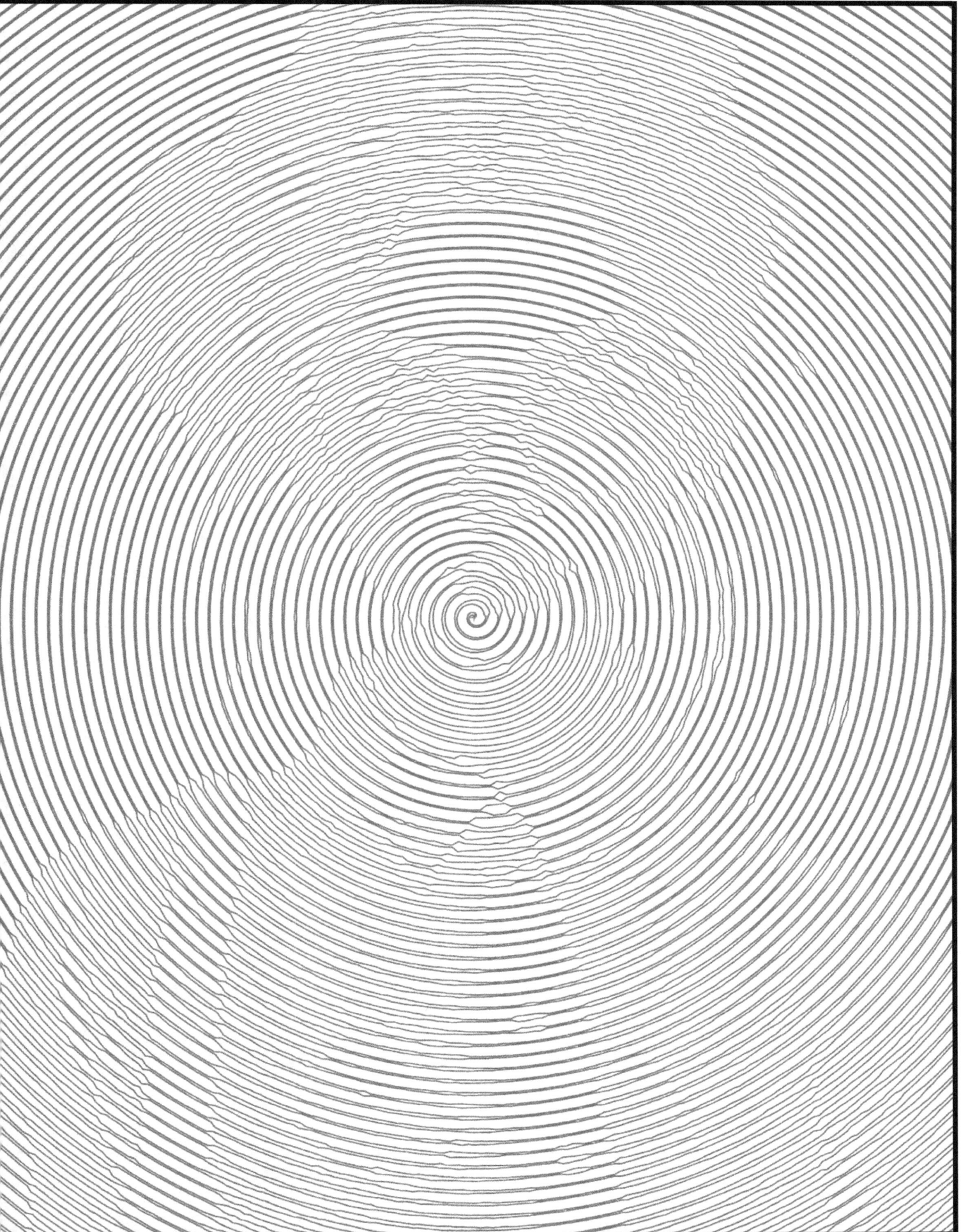

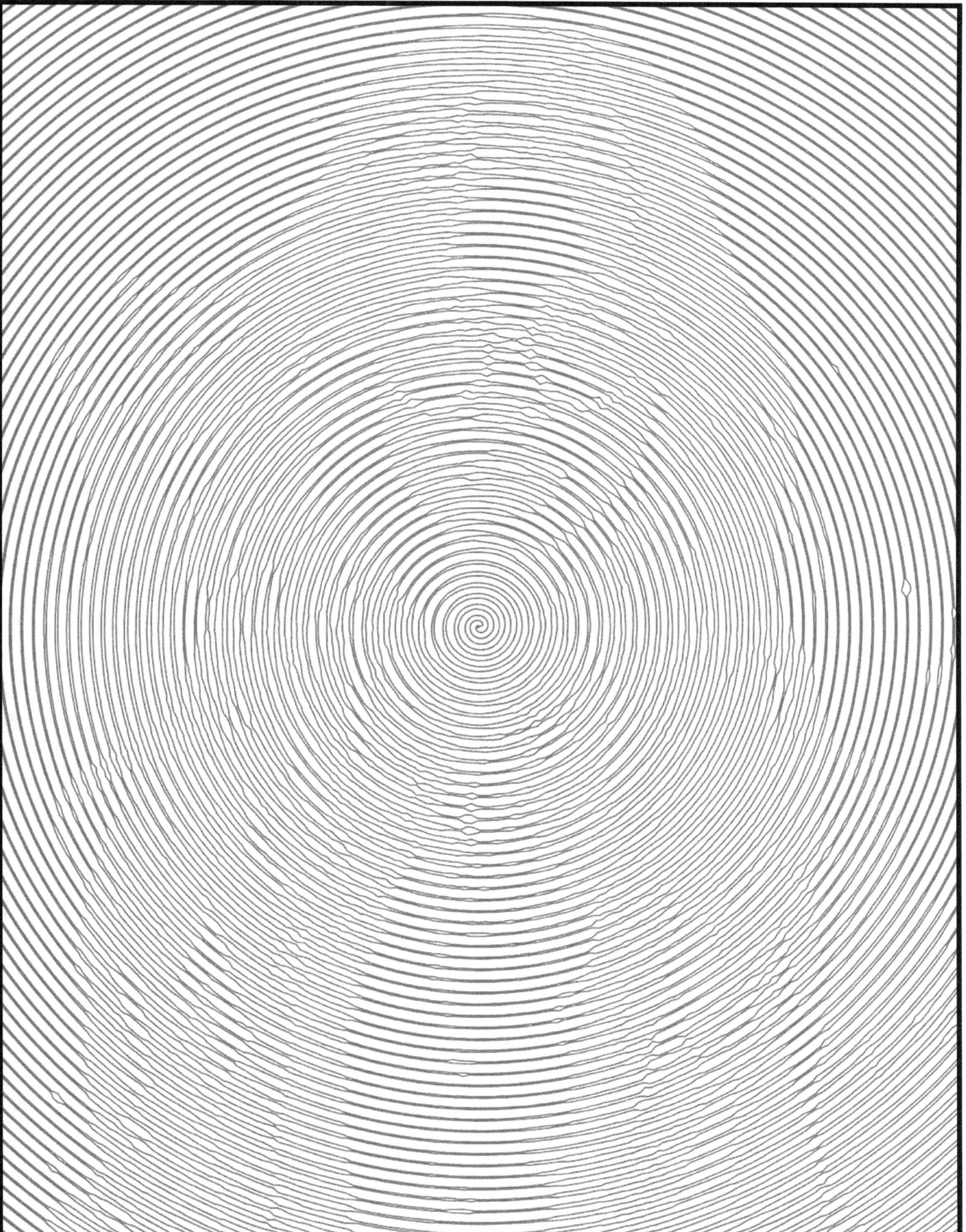

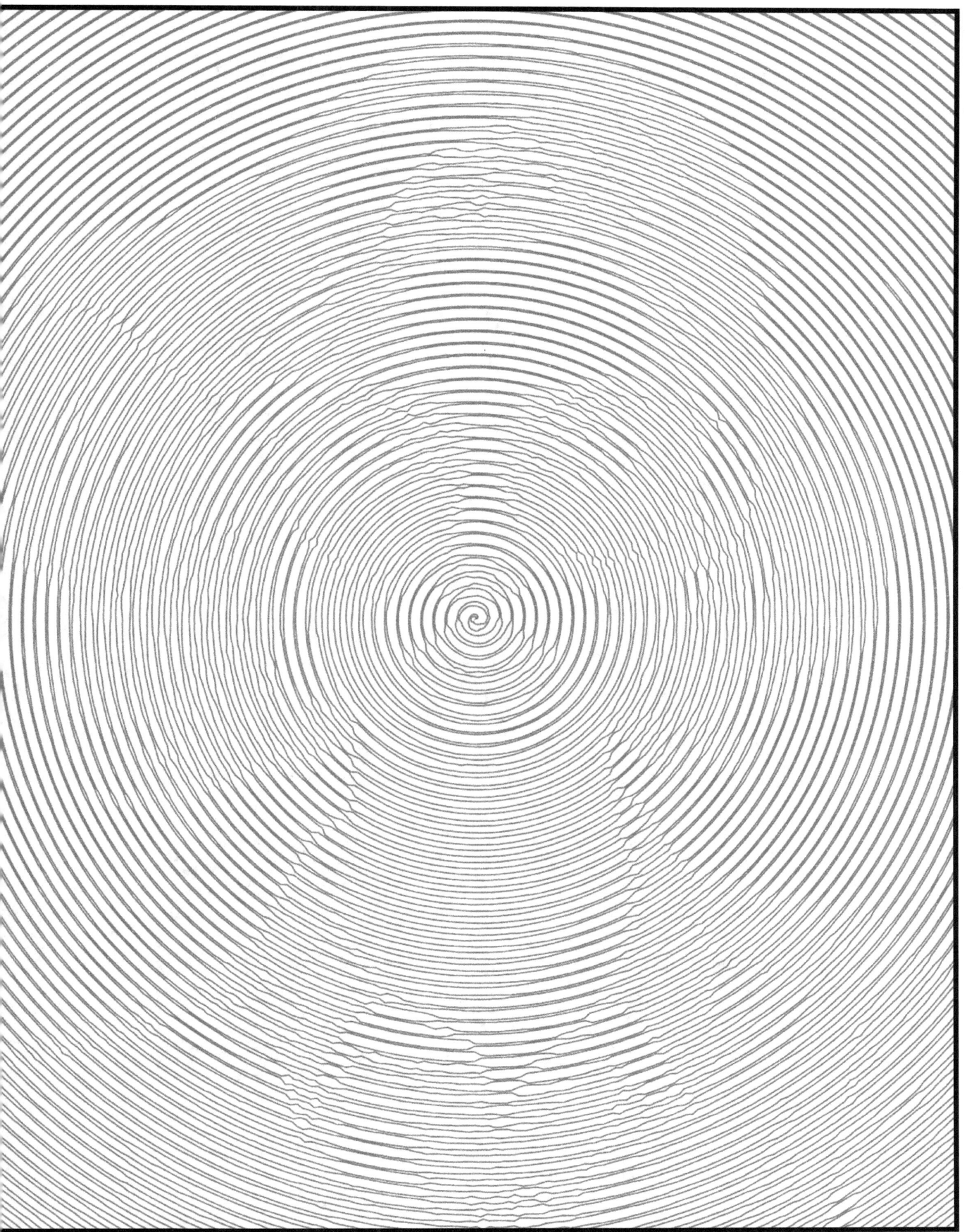

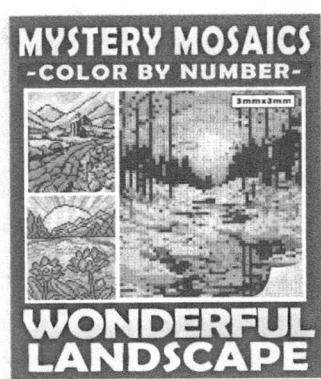

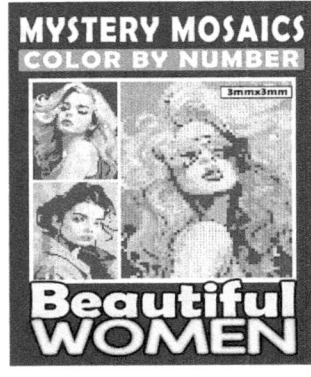

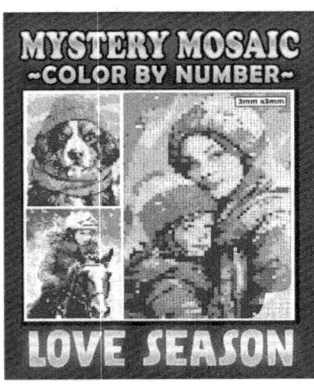

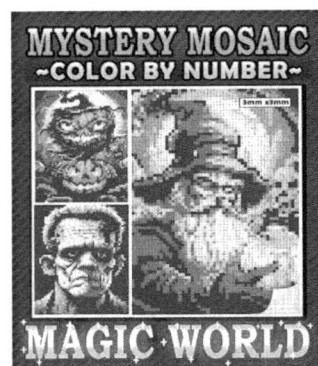

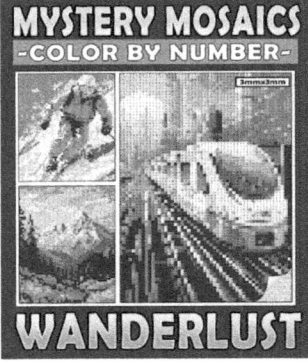

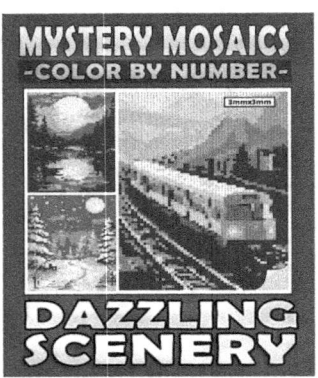

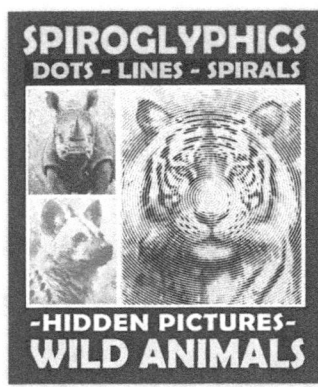

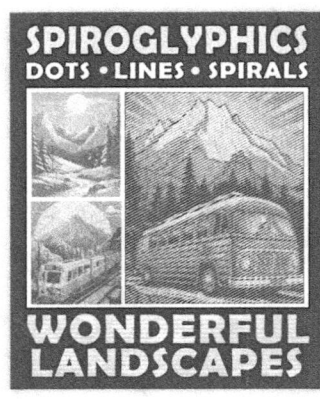

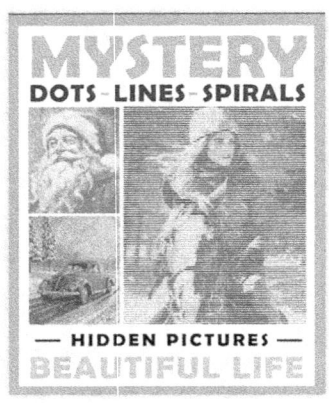

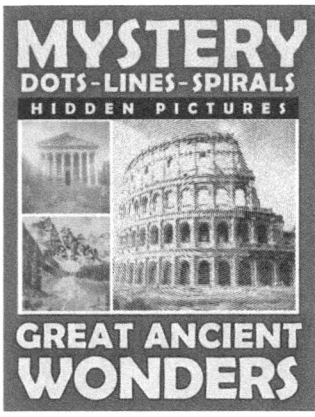

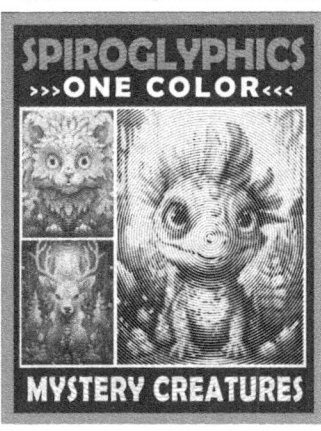

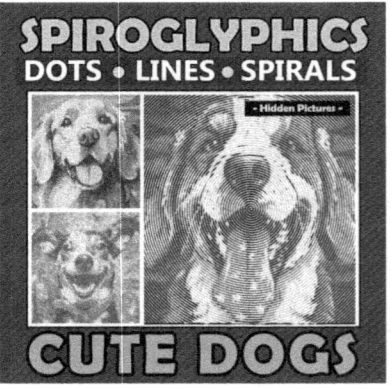

THANK YOU FOR CHOOSING US

TRY OUR OTHER COLORING BOOKS ON AMAZON

- MAXIMUS PRIME COLORING BOOKS-

Thank you for choosing this coloring book!
Please consider leaving a positive review on
Amazon. It would mean a lot to me and help
other customers find the book.
Your feedback is greatly appreciated!

★★★★★

♡ **Get Free Printable Coloring Pages** ♡
& Join Our Community!

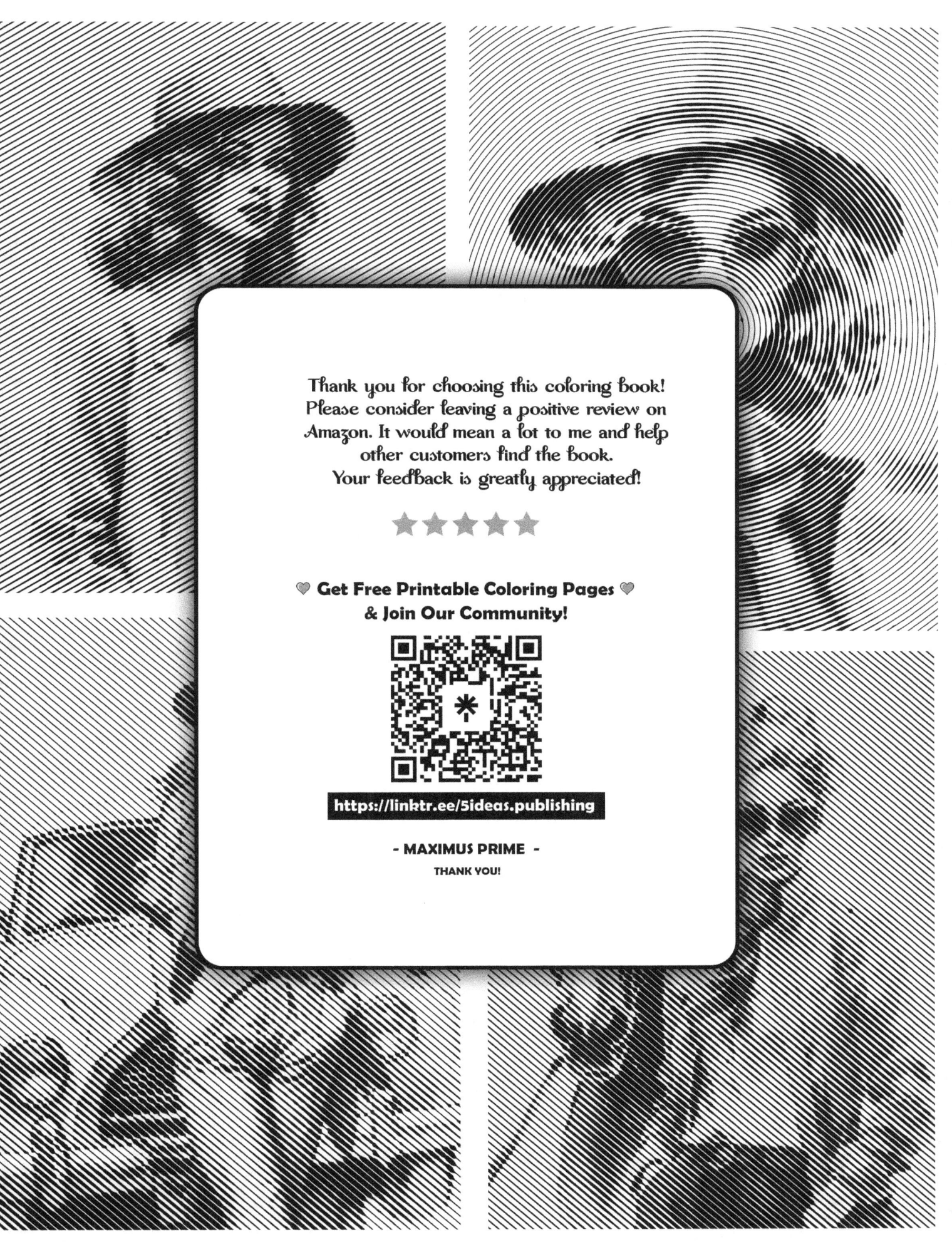

https://linktr.ee/5ideas.publishing

- MAXIMUS PRIME -

THANK YOU!